by Vita Jimenez
illustrated by Holly Cooper

Orlando Boston Dallas Chicago San Diego

Visit *The Learning Site!*

www.harcourtschool.com

What Are Crocodiles?

A crocodile is one of the largest living reptiles. There are 12 different kinds of crocodiles in the world today. An adult American crocodile is usually 12 feet long. The Nile crocodile usually grows to about 8 feet long. The longest one ever found, though, was almost 20 feet long.

Crocodiles have short legs. They look clumsy when they walk on solid ground. In the water, however, they are swift and almost graceful.

Crocodiles have lived on Earth for a very, very long time. Imagine the Earth 200 million years ago. It was the Age of Reptiles. Dinosaurs were roaming the land. Volcanoes were erupting lava into the air.

Along with the dinosaurs lived other reptiles, including crocodiles. In fact, crocodiles and alligators are the only reptiles that survived the dinosaur age. They are the last living relatives of the dinosaurs.

This book tells about a living crocodile named Croc. She was born in Africa, near the Nile River. Of course, she is a Nile crocodile.

Nile crocodiles can be found all over Africa except for the northern coast and in the Sahara Desert. We're going to learn about how Croc was born, what she eats, and how she hunts.

Baby Crocodiles

Croc's mother has just finished digging a hole deep in the ground. She will use the hole as a nest for her eggs.

She lays 40 eggs in the hole. The eggs look like goose eggs. They have hard white shells. She covers the eggs with sand so they are perfectly hidden.

Croc's mother stays nearby to guard her nest from predators. She guards against baboons, hyenas, and monitor lizards. They might like a crocodile egg omelet for brunch!

After three months, the baby crocodiles are ready to come out of their shells. They squeak and squawk inside their eggs. Their sounds come through the shells. The mother hears them and comes to the nest. These crocodiles are lucky because there are no enemies around.

One baby crocodile is first to break out of its shell. That's Croc! She's about 12 inches long at birth.

Now all of the eggs have hatched. Croc has 39 brothers and sisters. Their mother has to get her babies into the water. Amazingly, she carries them in her mouth. She does this by gently tossing each baby into the air and then catching it in her mouth.

The bottom of the mother's jaw forms a pouch in which to carry the babies. She carries the first group down to the peaceful safety of the water. Then she releases them and goes back time after time to carry the rest.

Adult crocodiles have no natural enemies, but baby crocodiles do. They can become food for hungry fish, birds, mammals, and even other reptiles. These babies are not in danger right now because their mother is nearby.

Once they are released, Croc and her siblings learn to catch their own food. At first they eat insects. When they get bigger, they start to eat frogs and fish. When they are adults, they can eat larger animals, including deer and zebra.

Crocodile Bodies

As time goes by, Croc grows bigger, longer, and smarter. She spends much of her life in the water. Her body is built for that kind of life. She has a thin body and webbed feet that are useful for swimming. She can also use her strong tail as a paddle. This helps her to be a powerful swimmer.

Croc can swim on the water's surface or dive underwater. When a crocodile dives, it closes up its throat, ears, and nose. This keeps the water out.

Like all reptiles, Croc is cold-blooded. That means her temperature is not always the same. A cold-blooded animal's temperature changes with the temperature of the air or water around it. If a reptile is in a cold place, its temperature goes down. If it goes to a warmer place, then its temperature goes up.

Croc warms up in the sun. If she gets too hot, she can go back into the water to cool off. Sometimes she holds her mouth open for a while. This lets air in to cool off her body.

How Crocodiles Hunt

Croc has grown up to be a very good hunter. She hunts best in the water. She eats turtles, snakes, birds, and fish. If she eats enough in one meal, she may not need to eat again for several days. If she does not get enough to eat, then she will soon hunt again.

Crocodiles cannot chew their food. They tear it into bite-size pieces and swallow it. Or, they may try to swallow it whole. Sometimes crocodiles lose a few teeth as they eat. New teeth grow in place of lost teeth.

Croc has good eyes and ears. She is also a quick hunter. She does not chase her prey. Instead, she sneaks up on it. Suppose she's hungry and sees an animal in the water. First, she slips into the water without making a sound. Then, she slowly floats upward until just her eyes and the top of her snout are showing. She is so quiet that her prey doesn't even know she's there.

Croc slips back underwater right before she attacks. She is very fast, and most animals have no chance to escape.

Endangered Crocodiles

The only real enemies that Croc has are people. Sometimes people kill crocodiles for their skin. Crocodile skins have been used to make things such as belts, boots, wallets, and handbags. These items are sold all over the world.

Some types of crocodile are already threatened. People need to do what they can to protect crocodiles and keep them from becoming extinct. Can you think of some ways crocodiles could be protected?

Luckily, some people are doing their best to make sure that crocodiles survive. In some parts of the world, scientists are helping out. They collect crocodile eggs and hatch them in protected areas. They keep the eggs safe from predators that might eat them. Scientists watch over the eggs just as the mother crocodile might. When the baby crocodiles are strong enough to live on their own, they are put back into the wild.

Back to Croc

Croc is eight years old now. Some crocodiles live to be much older than that. If she is lucky, she will be one of those crocodiles.

When Croc is ready to lay her eggs, she will make a nest just as her mother did. She'll lay her eggs, cover them, and stay nearby until they hatch.

After her babies are born, Croc will take them to the water. There, they will learn how to swim and hunt. Some of them will grow up and have babies of their own.

Glossary

cold-blooded a term for animals whose body temperature changes according to the temperature of their surroundings

endangered an animal or type of animal that is in danger of becoming extinct

extinct an animal that has died out and no longer exists

predator an animal that lives by hunting other animals for food

reptile a cold-blooded animal that crawls or creeps on the ground, has a backbone, has scaly skin, and lays eggs